Monster machine

Use your pen to follow the pipes all the way through the monster machine.

Try not to touch the sides.

START

Trace around all the boxes that contain a monster toy.

Usborne
Wipe-Clean
Pen Control

Use the wipe-clean pen to draw over all the dotted lines and finish the pictures and puzzles in this book.

Birdy

Slurpy

Pup

Illustrated by Kimberley Scott
Designed by Claire Ever. Words by Hannah Wood.

At the building site

Trace over all the straight lines, zig-zags, triangles, squares and rectangles at the building site.

In the sky

Trace over all the circles, wavy lines, curves, loops and swirls in the night sky.

FINISH

Beep! Beep!

Monster portraits

Draw the other halves of the monsters' faces to finish the monster portraits.

POTS

FLUTTER

SPUD

SPIKE

MUNCHY

Munchy's picnic

Join each group of dots to find out what
Munchy is eating on his picnic.

Slurpy's straw

Trace the curly straws to find out which monster drink belongs to Slurpy, then draw around the glass.

Spike   Spud   Slurpy

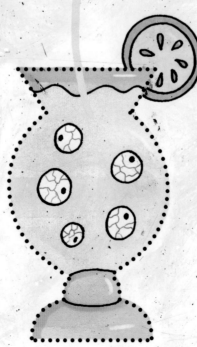

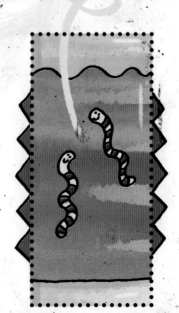

Underground monsters

Help this little monster find his way
back to his underground home.

FINISH

Fun at the fair

START

Trace over the roller coaster track as quickly as you can!

Join the dots to see what's at the fair.

TEST YOUR STRENGTH

FINISH

TICKETS

Going home

Use the wipe-clean pen to draw a route that Goggle could take to get home.

Goggle

START

Spud's house

Munchy's house

Pup's kennel

Pots' house

Spike's house

Slurpy's house

Goggle's house

Curly's house

Flutter's house

Birdy's tree

Flying kites

Join each set of dots to finish all the monster kites.

Trace the kite
strings to find out
which monster is
flying which kite.

In the garden

Add patterns to all the insects in Pots' garden.

Draw spots on the bugs.

Draw swirls on the snails.

Draw stripes
on the bees.

Draw zig-zags on the worms.

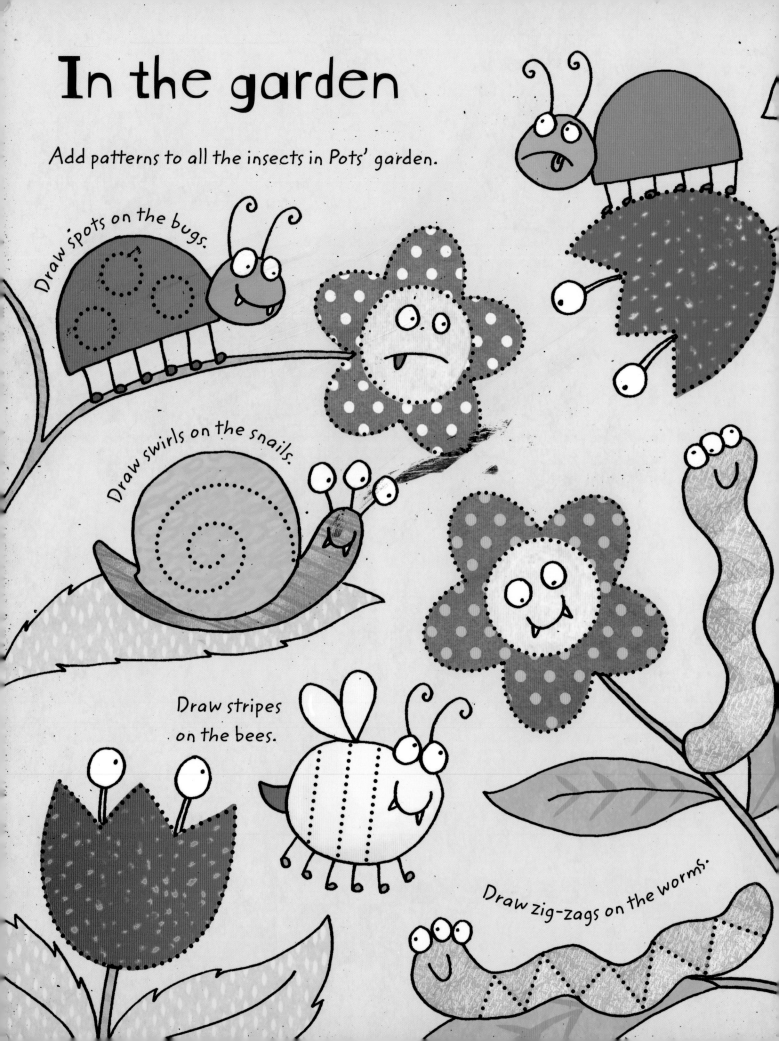